FINISHING LINE PRESS

www.finishinglinepress.com

The Last Bed

poems by

Lee Varon

Finishing Line Press
Georgetown, Kentucky

The Last Bed

ACKNOWLEDGMENTS

I'd like to thank my sons Jose and Jude for their love and support; my partner David for believing in me, and his expertise in the field of substance use disorder; my indispensable friend and computer guru, Sophia; and my Nar-anon support group, especially Pat, Mary Ellen, Felicia, Donna, Mary, Jane, Nancy, Anette, and many others. I'd also like to thank the many people who gave me feedback on earlier versions of these poems, including teacher and poet Tom Daley, and the poets Susan Donnelly, Jean Flanagan, and Alexis Ivy. Special thanks to Kathleen Aguero, Maryanne Frangules, and Timothy Gager for supporting "The Last Bed."

Publisher: Leah Huete de Maines
Editor: Christen Kincaid
Cover Art: Jude McElroy
Author Photo: Sophia Hasenfus
Cover Design: Elizabeth Maines McCleavy

Order online: www.finishinglinepress.com
also available on amazon.com

Author inquiries and mail orders:
Finishing Line Press
PO Box 1626
Georgetown, Kentucky 40324
USA

Contents

III
BIRDS

This book is dedicated to all those whose lives have been touched by substance use disorder.

I
AT THE SOUP KITCHEN

Extinct

So many languages have/ fallen off the edge of the world
—Lucille Clifton

This is where they used to roam
the ivory-billed woodpecker
through mangroves their missing poems—
a tinny trumpet flicker—
fallen off the edge of the world
into this shimmering void
a silence unfurled
into another forever destroyed.
100,000 souls overdosed
last year. Who remembers the shape of their hands
their lost poems that feed vanishing ghosts,
the stars that braided strands
of their hair? In 1935, someone recorded the ivory-billed bird
and what of the others?   Unheard.

I Know Your Name

for Colleen, 1989-2013

I know your name now,
I know you have no place
to sleep tonight.
I know you're so anxious
you can't come and sit
with the other guests
so I bring you a meal-to-go.
Don't give her money
someone says.
I give you chicken,
rice, an orange.

Your beauty is dissolving
into night—
smack, snow,
        taking you.

Heroin is white,
        but your lips are blue
and blue is seeping into the room
where you passed out last week,
the room where your head hit the floor,
blue dust wafting from the ceiling,
oozing from the floorboards
soaking your clothes.

Blue like your scarred veins
        pleading for oblivion.
At the end of your life
                a blue question mark.

She Remembers Her Lovers in Heaven

One gave me purple flowers
Five gave me valentines
Two saw halos above my head
Three said I love you
Four helped me make my sign:
HOMELESS   HUNGRY
One gave me inlaid pearl in dark wood
Three lost me in the woods
Two pierced my skin
One wanted me to play a bride in his movie
He gave me a birthday present—two bags of dope—
One found me—
         McDonald's, September, 2013.

Narcan Training

at the soup kitchen

1.
Beautiful in dreadlocks,
Ariel instructs us
in Rescue Breathing:
If lips are icy blue
and no response
when pressed on sternum: *Wake Up,
Wake Up!*

2.
They put him
in a cold
bathtub,
poured ice in

Someone went
to call 911
Someone said, *No
don't call!*

3.
Ariel shows us
how to take
caps off
Narcan Nasal Spray—
spray of mist,
          of light
of returning
from the dead

4.
I see him rise
from icy water
and live...
          and live again

5.
Ariel tells us
we have 60
maybe 90 minutes
to call for help:
Don't tell them
it's drugs,
they may not come.
Addicts
            are expendable

6.
My prayers
are like ripples
in ice frozen
            forever

7.
Ariel tells us
it can save a life,
this magic spray
I hold

waiting for him
            to return…

Grackles

Grackles fly over the doll factory.
Dolls reach out their stiff arms,

they know you're dead.
Someone sues Big Pharma—

too late for you.

At the back of the turquoise bodega
drug deals go down.

Even in jail you found things
to smile about

even if you smiled wistfully,
like someone who remembers red poppies

when they had eyes.

Addiction

All addictions arise from a longing for the infinite.
—A.S.

It's the last time she'll feel
that place of charred trees
opening again between her ribs,
scraping the inside of her skin
until she rises
throws on anything
rushes out into the black envelope of night
footfalls chasing behind.
She's not going to sit down
at the table
and eat loneliness
again
because it's over.
No more middle of the night
will come,
run out into snow
at any hour of where.
Not again her tongue
against the cold glass,
body warming
as morning arrives—
that yellow needle of light
and she can't turn away.

Remembering You

The room of my heart
is twilight,

some days blue.
I meet you there,

you wearing a coat
loud with drums

cymbals,
muffled cries,

addiction
then …

I write your name
with small sticks,

set them afire,
take the smoke home.

To the Needle Exchange Worker

for Karen Hale, whose daughter, Alysa Ivy, died of a heroin overdose

Some days you're lead-footed
lumbering like a sleepwalker
waiting to be woken.
Other days, your toes skim the ground
and wings push from inside
your bent shoulders.

You never know which it will be
but you go anyhow

into the underground of trap houses
with your packet of shiny needles
your small slivers of hope

as you push down the memory
of your dead child;
try to save the one before you—
ragged hangnails, bruise beneath their hair.

Here, you know love
and you know what it is to be lost.

How Are You?

Throngs stream through the church door.
I offer apples, bananas,
above the roar of another Tuesday:
And how are you?

Always, the question hangs
among pushing hands, bleating cries.
He works with addicts, the homeless,
and who will he save tonight

as he sits and stirs
his coffee dispensing help with dinner?
A madrigal of voices
in the desperate air rises

falls, rises. Brief moments on the rim
of sanity tilt my heart toward him,
toward corridors of hope
where everything in the room is rinsed of dust,

is shining. The wild moon
still pushes against blackened screens.
Another overdose in the bathroom,
a constant winter

and still the language of love
seeps in,
settles into the crevice of night
as throngs stream through the church door.

At Red Rock Beach

Snails coil into secrets
as planes fly low.

I step among the rusted fishhooks,
derelict dreams.

By the tidal pool
someone's overdosed.

This is what I know
about ghosts.

Big Pharma

They invented a white pill—
a different kind of misery.

It took away slivers of shrapnel
imbedded in muscle.
It took away a twisted kidney,
a mind running through loneliness.

Then they cut back.

For the same money
you could buy 4 bags of heroin
just as potent,
fentanyl laced.

Ten years
scribbled names on prescription pads
then they cut back…

you learned about heroin in detox:
safe and effective for long term use.

What Happens

Kam Killsfirst is studying Comanche at Comanche Nation College.
Only 25 people nationwide speak Comanche, down from about 15,000
in the late 1800s.

What happens when a language slowly dies?
Is love spoken differently?
Hate?
Does the blue bowl shining on a table shine differently?
Or simply disappear?

I heard in Mexico there are only two people alive
who speak Ayapaneco, *The True Voice,*
and they're not speaking to each other.

What disappears in the space between them
besides sunflower stalks and evening's gray moths?
There are different ways to say *Death:*
All are permanent.

II
THE LAST BED

Kindergarten

First day of kindergarten
               in your sweater vest,
clutching your dinosaur lunchbox,
                 smile wide.
Who was to know
the Tyrannosaurus and Triceratops
                would take over your life
ravenous, unforgiving?
And me
               clutching my camera,
trembling at the world
               you are about to enter.

Rainbow

A rainbow arches over Everett's
scrap metal junkyard
groaning under its own rusting weight.

A lone man pees
against a fence.
I don't use the word *bum* anymore.

I've run out of red crayons,
of hope and its synonyms.
I collect black crosses.

We drive to detox,
you huddled
in the suicide seat.

One by one you blew through
jobs, rooms,
toothbrushes, prayers.

What's this rainbow for?
God blessing your next try or

God bringing you home?

How Many Times?

The sky cracks like a broken fortune cookie.
       Is this your life's final draft
shuddering in a homeless shelter
dope sick?
Can't you go back?
       Put in another tape?

At the Wilderness Program
they drove you into the desert where you camped for 6 weeks
       lost your name,
became *Coyote,*
        sparked fires from juniper bark.

I rented a car
       drove 90 on deserted roads
           dodging rabbits at dusk.

After running 3 miles you crossed the finish line.

How was I to know there is
              no finish line?
Endless detoxes, holding tanks,
       walls scoured of graffiti,
           cigarette butts overflowing coffee cans,
locked doors, transition centers, halfway houses
       where drugs still seep in and tears
              await
as I sip from the straw of hope
following the filigree of an angel's wing.

ER

At .30 one is in a stupor
has little comprehension   where they are,
can suddenly pass out….be difficult to awaken.

A nurse brings Librium
               for severe withdrawal.

At .40 one probably is in a coma—
nerve centers controlling heartbeat,
respiration   slowing down
slowing
        slowing
               s l o w i n g
                           down.

You
        are
a heavy wing
            that cannot fly.

Juncos at the ER

Hummingbirds
have departed.

Dusky juncos
arrive like a relapse.

Life is more
than euphoric desolation.

I want to grab your torn shirt
your trembling hands…

It takes forever for the nurses to come…
They have heart attacks, strokes…

Juncos show up as spirit guides
when you need to be able to survive in every situation.

The Call

I've waited for it
for years…
Black bud of death
always opening.

Your memorial already planned
in English
and Spanish for the other side of the family.

A mother told me her son
visits her in dreams
speaking their childhood language.

In dreams will you remember
the language we spoke?

Epidemic

Pope Francis is the first pope
to take the name
of the patron saint of animals.

In this time of dying
the business of wakes
and coffins is doing quite well.

Some release white doves for healing
some for peace.
Pope Francis ended this practice.

When the world's heart breaks,
he advised:
Pray to the God of surprises.

Dunlin

Its breeding plumage so bright
it looks like a different bird

just as you in rehab,
or soon after,

glowed
with light

only to twist again,
dun-colored, into addiction.

I wanted to keep that light—
you and I circling the rehab

by the horse stables,
tears for a roommate who OD'd.

Before leaving I stand before memorials—
Miss you Daddy/ See you in Heaven/Our forever angel—

hearts cracked in two.
Retrieve my car keys, cell phone, head home.

Stop time, God!
I yell in my empty car

as traffic slows on the Mass Pike
and ahead, blue lights flash.

Dreaming

Keep living like you're dreaming
       —Jason Wright

I will always keep dreaming you

not homeless
not slipping beneath icy water
no ambulance called
not dragged under palm trees
glare of sun
too many skaters on the boardwalk

Dreaming no officer
picked you up
blacked out incoherent
phone stolen
homeless shelter Ward's Island
bunkmate chattering all night

Keep dreaming no rats
scurry around you
Everett junkyard
liquor oozing from your pores
last pawned trinket my mother's cross—
turquoise center—

Keep dreaming you don't break in
steal everything

living like you're dreaming
running dreaming outrunning death
in your cloak of black leaves

Thanksgiving

This Thanksgiving you're sober.
Your words aren't slurred,
eyes aren't bloodshot;
you and your brother tease me about my driving.
Slowly,
I reach our destination. Out past Holyoke,
Lee, Hudson, to Millerton.
Silos, still groups of cows and sheep
replace shopping malls, service areas.
Hemlock, fir, and white birch
replace maple and oak.
Breathing replaces
the clenched chest, strained muscles;
I walk into the shadowed hills.
Just for today.

Conversation

The dark halls of anger
and sadness
lie empty.

I watch a slice of light
rise in the sky—
this sliver of moon
called *Future.*

You could have one.

Mother's Day

A day of running.
Running from silence,
the phone that doesn't ring

the empty mailbox.
Running past aisles
of hallmark cards,

turning off the radio:
Not too late to send your mother
…long-stemmed

Running
from flowers   red

running. Waiting for
the moon to rise.

Going to the YMCA

You leave your Red Sox cap
on the dining room table
this chilly spring day.

I take you to your new room,
room 1155 at the West Side Y.
The window won't open—
glued shut around the AC unit.
A deterrent to suicide?
From the 11th floor—
a line of yellow taxis
careens down Broadway.

You fall on your cot,
eyes closed,
a circle of fluorescent light
tinges your skin green.
On a scrap of paper
you copy a list—
names, birthdays
of friends, family
(*for safe keeping,* you say).

I'm glad you can't see my face
                    as I walk away.

Nighthawk

Some pictures in my bird book
(c. 1949) are missing.

You've been missing
for a long time.

Even when you were here
you were missing.

I bring back no words
from my sighting of you

at night
crossing 72nd street.

In my book the nighthawk is missing.
The nighthawk is constantly

in the air. Flying
in a zig-zag path.

You, sleepless and
hollow-eyed crossing 72nd street

falling down
the metro stairs.

Unseen, I watch you.
Nighthawks dive and bank

as they feed on flying insects. You—
diving and banking as you move forward

like a low flying bird
in the crepuscular evening.

Both display cryptic coloration
gray white buff blue—mottled.

Now deleted
from the pages of my life.

Tattoos

Love is the voice under all silences,
—e.e. cummings

Imprinted on your skin
tattoos—black green gold sleeves
encircling your arms,
ghosts of the departed: *LAURA RIP*
in blue letters,
and *HAPPY,* your roommate in Long Beach
who never smiled, found with
a needle in his arm,
Match.com flickering on the screen.
This lost assembly
where love   exhausted
love   derailed   is still love—
a hum between syllables
under everything
love torn yet   still love,
love whispers   under all silences.

In Detox

You had a seizure last night
broke your nose,
stitches above black eyes.

Your eighth try.
I send angels to your side.

At Pacific Beach you wandered
into waves, your glasses
flowed away among surfers.

Jacaranda blooms
stained the sidewalks lavender
like your body bruised with pain.

Ashen clouds strewn
over Boston's skyline—did you come home
to die?

Wherever you go
I never stop missing you.

The Last Bed

Driving to Boston Medical
                                you vomit in a plastic bag.
I keep my eyes on the road.
You're shaking
         the car shakes,
                  stars even shake.

No, this isn't the first time you've
                                  blinked back from death.
After 10, I stopped counting.

The intake worker calls around:
no beds   no beds
                  maybe one bed in Worcester.

You know there's an epidemic, he sighs.

Past midnight, a young man
                stumbles in
despair smoldering in the creases of his jacket.
Any beds?

I want to bury this man
           beneath the unplowed snow.
Doesn't he know the last bed is yours?

How many times has his mother buried him?
Outside, stars swirl faster.

I want that bed.
            That bed is ours! I scream   don't scream.

The worker coughs…tells him
You'll need to go to a shelter,
come back tomorrow.

I know his tomorrow may never come…

but through blood and splinters

I grip the edge
of the last bed.

The Medium

Can you believe and not believe?
What is the color of hope?
What are the limits of the expanding universe?

Can you take a bone from your body
and make a new person?

Theresa Caputo claims spirits have followed her
since childhood.
As she ate her Cheerios for breakfast,
one would emerge from the wall.
She's on a first name basis with many.

Tonight, she holds the mic: The stillborn baby
speaks, the departed drug addict sends kisses.

Whatever may be fake, the burials are real.

The crying couple waves goodbye to their child.
The mother who couldn't open a photo album
laughs at the memory of her son's joke.

From Theresa's open palm
light—once condensed to the size of a thimble—
spills forth, slaying us in the spirit

Moments

They say geographical cures don't work.
I was learning the wrong language all along.
I took you to a cottage beneath black palms
orange raspberries beneath our window

sweet jasmine curling into crushing hope.
You surfed silver highways looking for something never found.

Do the language of love and addiction intersect somewhere?
I sold the cottage and came home. When I returned it was
plowed under.

Even the black palms gone. Jasmine came
to remind me we'd had moments of happiness.

His Mother

His mother wondered
if he'd prefer an open or closed casket,
red cherry or rustic oak.
And who would give the eulogy?
Would they post it on YouTube?

Speech bubbles above our heads
are interchangeable.

Buzzwords:
She/He went out
The Call
Better Place
                    and so on…

My son, there are no spare seasons and
forever is a long way home.

Addict's Mother

Philip Seymour Hoffman's grieving mother Marilyn O'Connor arrived in Manhattan today
— *Mail Online*, February, 24, 2012

The addict's mother is hidden
in the fine print.

She's filled with lavender tears.
She lies awake all night,

telephone cords grow from her body.
No one will answer.

Thanks…

with gratitude for my support groups

for accompanying me
on this lonely journey
to losing everything to
regaining small bits and
losing again
on this roller coaster that is loving
an addict—a word
we no longer use but
what shall I say? *Loving*
the person hating the disease?
Loving a person who is sick as we
become sick with worry   with fear.
There was always the cottage
with its dark palms and golden raspberries;
I clung to that
waiting for a boy I once knew to open the gate
waiting became a life, became breathing
became this moment (too).

Enabler

At school
She finished his science project
making the volcano
out of red paper-mâché
because it wasn't worth
arguing about.
She left for work
and let him sleep all day,
school became optional.

She wondered how he got all that money
for video games,
            cigarettes, new sneakers…

When he was older
she told his boss he was sick
when he was hung over.
She picked him up at the hospital
after the cops found him
passed out,
people walking around him
like a pile of old clothes.
She gave him one more chance
and another
one more.
She paid for detox
rehab,
insurance,
weeks in the wilderness,
for flights to new beginnings
(Some with ocean views).
She let him swear
break things
take things,
said not again
and it happened again.
She blamed herself:
a mountain of reproach
rose before her,

She prayed for change
and changed
one hard thing at a time,
like obsidian
slicing skin.
She used the mallet
of anger
of fear
of hurt
and at the end
she was left
with this fine powder
of sadness.

Amend

There was one amend she never made.
He was a baby; she left him alone in his crib.
It was only for half an hour.
He was a sound sleeper she told herself.

She was going in search of a man
who drank too much
as he would one day
drink too much.

She never forgot that night. She didn't remember
if she found the man but she remembers
the feel of her hands gripping the wheel
as she pulled away from the curb past midnight.

She remembers the hairs on the back of her neck
slick with sweat, her teeth chattering in August.
Sometimes, she replays that night: A semi hits her
head on. She loses her keys. The tire goes flat.

In the cell-phoneless night he lay in a black room
his small fists uncurling into neglect.
She never left him again. She wanted that night
to erase itself. Like secret writing

that disappears in bright sunlight. But she knows
she must eat her regret
despite the gristle,
the slivers of bone.

Phoenix

Where did the mother's go?
To what rough god do we pray?
—Miriam Greenspan

she shows me
the postcard from Neptune cremation services
advertising a free lunch and information seminar:

Outback Steakhouse
or Olive Garden.
Her son OD'd again.

He's the Lazarus of Narcan.
The phoenix
of 2nd chances.

If one attends the lunch *and* the seminar
they can win
a weekend getaway.

She'd like something warm.
Tropical.
Where nothing ever freezes.

Spring

Six months recovery—Spring
startles with unexpected crocuses

white snowdrops
brief visit

violets scatter
in long frozen ground.

I think of the other mothers…

if it's spring here
can't it be spring everywhere?

Eighteen Months, Recovery

You take your girlfriend to detox
as I once drove you along the potholes of Mass. Ave
to Boston Medical.

I have a video we took that night—
your hands shaking, skin
hanging on depleted bones.

You give your girlfriend a pink rose.
You give her kisses you've been saving for years.
I wish I could spare you the urgent truth:

She loves someone more than you.
Someone who stuffs promises in her suitcase,
someone with a voice like liquid caramel,

a nomad who goes by different names:
Juice, Tar, Mud, sometimes just *H.*
The trustee of hopelessness

holds her hand and whispers, *Come,*
come into the shadow of no memories,
the fortuity of my embrace.

Seagulls

The seagulls look down
on another summer of bleaching.

The *rainforests of the sea*
are dying.

It can be a gradual process
like addiction.

Olive green, pale yellow, golden brown,
florescent red—gone.

Denial is easy.
I kept thinking you'd be ok

as your downward slide continued
and we headed into another bad year.

High above gulls cry
holding to hope

that corals can recover,
regain their color.

At the Garden, on Your Eighth Anniversary of Recovery

You wait for me as I greet
our oak tree, our Carolina Wren high in the branches.
At the garden wild strawberries redden
beneath a tangle of green, among

lettuce in small clumps, yellow tomato flowers
all beckoning, waiting.
Years ago, we sped our bikes
around this pond, crashing against each other

as we barreled into our lives. How many years not talking
barely talking, arguing, accusing, then just missing?
I watch for a bird I thought would never arrive
just like I never thought you'd make it to 40.

We water the garden, home for pizza, salad,
dessert—this bowl of wild strawberries.

III
BIRDS

Outside, Crows Swoop Down on Pigeons

Watch out for the bathroom,
yells the cashier at Au Bon Pain.
Over 500 people use it every day.
He's had it with all the *junkies*
who litter his sidewalk.

I'd like to put them all in one room
let them fight over a glass of water! Ha!

Outside, black crows swoop down—
pushing pigeons aside—
flap wings and caw.

My child is one of those
thirsty,
stumbling from the bathroom
camouflaged as a patron.

Outside, beneath rain, orange syringes
litter the alleys like garish pick-up-sticks
while crows, chests puffed out, march
up and down the slick streets.

Kestrel

With pointed wings
and fan-shaped tail
the Kestrel flies
at speeds of
39 mph

The males have
gray-blue heads
the color of a bruise

The Kestrel can dive
for prey
at 200 mph
This is how
fentanyl swoops down—

One minute you're
moving among the brackish
waters of life—

the next gone.

Peacocks

The peacocks
strut their luminous wares.

Wherever you go
their purple moons tremble with promise.

When you sleep
they catch your dreams in snares.

They peck your bright hopes,
leaving

only
death's dope.

Pileated Woodpecker

The Pileated Woodpecker is drilling again.
I hear it across the pond.
Its crimson head
leaps from trunk to trunk.

Is this what trying to stay clean is like?
The beak of addiction gives no peace.
It must be heard.
It will uncover one's weaknesses

like tiny grubs
trying to remain invisible
as they burrow
for cover.

The Pileated Woodpecker
has a specialized beak;
it can peck 12,000 times a day
at 15 miles per hour.

Warbler

Sun gilded your hair
as the yolk-colored warbler
flitted among bees.

I ignored the bruises
like blue delphiniums
circling your arm.

Mandelstam wrote that he was
"wearied to death of life…"
Is this how it was at the end?

The intensity of your misfortune
spread across the violet sky.
"The earth buzzes," he wrote, "with metaphor."

From the Gulag he begged his wife
for a package of warm clothes.
You wanted to plant a garden,

a new beginning, you said.
I sent you seeds.
Neither package arrived.

Cedar Waxwings

More than 5,000 kids have died from fentanyl in the U.S. since 1999.
—CBS News 9-18-23

I knew you would arrive
like the stories of children walking into heaven.

I went looking for you
to no avail.

My beautiful ones, the color of cinnamon,
with your shrill cries

behind your black masks
are you crying?

At last, you arrive—a museum
of commotion among the strawberries.

Egret

It strides through the marsh at Belle Isle
as planes glide into Logan.
The president hasn't mentioned drugs
since the Covid Lockdown began mid-March
yet still addicts die
and more every day;

they walk through the reeds
like Snowy Egrets.

Their ghosts stride through tall grasses.
I saw one moving sidewise in the birch grove,
beckoning.

Great Blue Heron

Some believe spirits of the dead
return in birds.

I found one wading in the reeds and cattails
along Little Pond today—
more gray than blue,

a rustling,
an intention,
                    wading

then lifting
gray into blue clouds,
wingspan five or six feet across

cruising,
its blade-like bill
parting the veil between two worlds.

Geese

Sometimes a long-dead friend stops by for a while.
—Wisława Szymborska

I climb into the branches
& disappear into the white pear blossoms
                              for a while.

I listen to the low honking of geese
flying through opaque clouds
                              for a while.

I pretend your hand turning the doorknob
as you come to see me will last
                              for a while.

Vigil with Hummingbirds

At night their photos are projected
on buildings.

We hold our lit cell phones
to the black sky and pray.

Someone loved each,
washed their dead bodies in dreams.

They want you to remember their names
their faces, before the addiction set in,

to know
they'll return

like hummingbirds—
fly through the missing pages of our lives.

THE END

ACKNOWLEDGMENTS

The author would like to thank the editors of the following journals, where these poems first appeared, sometimes in earlier versions.

Bagel Bard Anthology: "Phoenix"
Breakwater Review: "What Happens"
Burningword Literary Journal: "Grackles," "Peacocks," "Eighteen Months Recovery"
Connecticut River Review: "Kindergarten"
Crab Creek Review: "Extinct"
Constellations: A Journal of Poetry and Fiction: "Warbler"
Crosswinds Poetry Journal: "Remembering you"
Dash Literary Journal: "Big Pharma"
Flights: "Kestrel"
High Plains Literary Review: "Addiction" with the title "It"
Madness Muse Addiction/Recovery Anthology: "Rainbow," "Tattoos," "The Last Bed," "Outside, Crows Swoop Down on Pigeons"
Muddy River Poetry Review: "In Detox"
Oddball Magazine: "Going to the YMCA", "Thanksgiving," "To the Needle Exchange Worker" under the title "What it is to be Lost"
Prick of the Spindle: "Narcan Training"
The Red Letter Poems Project # 44: "Juncos at the ER"
The Red Letter Poems Project: "Dunlin" and "Geese"
Right Hand Pointing: "At Red Rock Beach," "Conversation"
The Somerville Times: "Dreaming"
Spare Change News: "Why?" under the title "Colleen"
A Stone's Throw: "She Remembers Her Lovers in Heaven"
Toe Good: "His Mother"
Two Hawks Quarterly: "Amend"
The Willow Review: "Enabler"
Vagabond City: "Nighthawk"

Lee Varon is a writer and social worker who has personal experience with members of her own family who have substance use disorder. She is a co-editor of *Spare Change News Poems: An Anthology by Homeless People and Those Touched by Homelessness* and author of the children's books: *My Brother is Not a Monster: A Story of Addiction and Recovery* (2021) and *A Kids Book About Overdose* (2024).

Milton Keynes UK
Ingram Content Group UK Ltd.
UKHW031159251124
451529UK00004B/364

9 798888 387931